CLIFFHANGERS

Sue Palmer
Alison Kilpatrick
Patricia McCall

Oliver & Boyd

Acknowledgments

The authors and publishers are grateful to the following for permission to reproduce extracts from copyright material:

Allison & Busby, from *The Worst Witch* by Jill Murphy; The Bodley Head, from *Tales of a Fourth Grade Nothing* by Judy Blume; Jonathan Cape Ltd, from *The Enormous Crocodile* by Roald Dahl; Dell Publishing Co Inc, from *Chocolate Fever* by Robert Kimmel Smith; J. M. Dent & Sons Ltd, from *A Pony in the Luggage* by Gunnel Linde; Faber & Faber Ltd, from *Clever Polly and the Stupid Wolf* by Catherine Storr; Hamish Hamilton Ltd, from *Saturday Shillings* by Penelope Farmer and *Hide Till Daytime* by Joan Phipson; Hodder & Stoughton Ltd, from *Lion at Large* by Richard Parker; and Julia MacRae Books, from *Dinner Ladies Don't Count* by Bernard Ashley.

The authors would also like to thank the children and staff of Comiston Primary School, Edinburgh; Caddonfoot Primary School, Galashiels and Stenwood Elementary School, Virginia, USA, for all their help; and Jeannette Perry, Ishbel Fraser and Graham Harding, without whom *Cliffhangers* could not have been written.

Illustrated by Nancy Bryce, Peter Chapel,
John Harrold and Maggie Ling.

Oliver & Boyd
Robert Stevenson House
1—3 Baxter's Place
Leith Walk
Edinburgh EH1 3BB

A Division of Longman Group UK Ltd

ISBN 0 05 003631 9

First published 1983
Fifth impression 1987

Produced by Longman Group (FE) Ltd
Printed in Hong Kong

Contents

Introduction

In *Cliffhangers* you will find extracts from ten exciting fiction books written for people of your age. We hope that in the *Cliffhanger* extracts and the sections called "Other Good Reads" you will find many books that you would like to read for yourself. The "Other Good Reads" are coded with stars – one star means that it is quite an easy book to read, two means that it is of medium difficulty, and three stars means that it's better left to good readers. Choose books that you know you'll be able to read quite easily – then you can relax and enjoy the story. If you like a book, then it's a good idea to look out for other books by the same author.

It should be easy to get hold of the books – try your school or class library or your local lending library. You can join the local library simply by filling in a form. You will then receive two or three tickets. It is completely free, unless you keep a book out for too long. Since all the *Cliffhanger* books are paperbacks, you may even want to go out and buy them!

Sometimes you enjoy a book more if you think about it and talk about it. You may even be able to understand your own opinion and your own experiences better when you come across something similar in books. This is why we ask you to discuss the extracts either with a small group or with the whole class. The discussion should help you to work out what is happening (or is about to happen) and why the characters act as they do. You will also have the chance to talk about things that have happened to you, and your thoughts about various subjects. There is no "right" or "wrong" answer. Your ideas and the way you explain them are what counts. Often you will find that you get ideas from what other people say, so remember that it is important to listen as well as to speak.

All the sections in *Cliffhangers* should be enjoyable – reading, talking and activities – so have fun and Good Reading!

1 The Enormous Crocodile
by Roald Dahl

Roald Dahl was born in Wales. During the Second World War he was a fighter pilot in the RAF. He has written lots of books — some for children and some for grown-ups. He has also often been on TV, talking about his stories.

Roald Dahl is married to an actress called Patricia Neal, and they have four children.

* * * * * * * * * * *

In the biggest brownest muddiest river in Africa, two crocodiles lay with their heads just above the water. One of the crocodiles was enormous. The other was not so big.

"Do you know what I would like for my lunch today?" the Enormous Crocodile asked.

"No," the Notsobig One said. "What?"

The Enormous Crocodile grinned, showing hundreds of sharp white teeth. "For my lunch today," **he said,** "I would like a nice juicy little child."

"I never eat children," **the Notsobig One said.** "Only fish."

"Ho, ho, ho!" **cried the Enormous Crocodile.** "I'll bet if you saw a fat juicy little child paddling in the water over there at this very moment, you'd gulp him up in one gollop!"

"No, I wouldn't," **the Notsobig One said.** "Children are too tough and chewy. They are tough and chewy and nasty and bitter."

"*Tough* and *chewy!*" **cried the Enormous**

Crocodile. "*Nasty* and *bitter!* What awful tommy-rot you talk! They are juicy and yummy!"

"They taste so bitter," **the Notsobig One said,** "you have to cover them with sugar before you can eat them."

"Children are bigger than fish," **said the Enormous Crocodile.** "You get bigger helpings."

"You are greedy," **the Notsobig One said.** "You're the greediest croc in the whole river."

"I'm the bravest croc in the whole river," **said the Enormous Crocodile.** "I'm the only one who dares to leave the water and go through the jungle to the town to look for little children to eat."

"You've only done that once," **snorted the Notsobig One.** "And what happened then? They all saw you coming and ran away."

"Ah, but today when I go, they won't see me at all," **said the Enormous Crocodile.**

"Of course they'll see you," **the Notsobig One said.** "You're so enormous and ugly, they'll see you from miles away."

The Enormous Crocodile grinned again, and his terrible sharp teeth sparkled like knives in the sun. "Nobody will see me," he said, "because this time I've thought up secret plans and clever tricks."

"*Clever tricks?*" cried the Notsobig One. "You've never done anything clever in your life! You're the stupidest croc on the whole river!"

"I'm the cleverest croc on the whole river," the Enormous Crocodile answered. "For my lunch today I shall feast upon a fat juicy little child while you lie here in the river feeling hungry. Goodbye."

The Enormous Crocodile swam to the side of the river, and crawled out of the water.

A gigantic creature was standing in the slimy oozy mud on the river-bank. It was Humpy-Rumpy, the Hippopotamus.

"Hello, hello," said Humpy-Rumpy. "Where on earth are you off to at this time of day?"

"I have secret plans and clever tricks," said the Crocodile.

"Oh dear," **said Humpy-Rumpy.** "I'll bet you're going to do something horrid."

The Enormous Crocodile grinned at Humpy-Rumpy and said:

> *I'm going to fill my hungry empty tummy*
> *With something yummy yummy yummy*
> *yummy!"*

"What's so yummy?" **asked Humpy-Rumpy.**

"Try to guess," **said the Crocodile.** "It's something that walks on two legs."

"You don't mean . . . " **said Humpy-Rumpy.**
"You don't *really* mean you're going to eat a
little child?"

"Of course I am," **said the Crocodile.**

"Oh, you horrid greedy grumptious brute!"
cried Humpy-Rumpy. "I hope you get caught
and cooked and turned into crocodile soup!"

**The Enormous Crocodile laughed out loud at
Humpy-Rumpy. Then he waddled off into the
jungle.**

* * * * * * * * * * * * *

A. Talking about the story

1. (a) What does the Enormous Crocodile look
       like? Find all the words that describe him in
       the story.
   (b) What sort of "person" do you think he is?
       Find clues in the story which tell you about
       his character.

2. (a) Why does the Enormous Crocodile want to
       eat a little child for lunch?
   (b) Why does the Notsobig Crocodile think that
       eating a child is not a good idea?

3. Do you think the Enormous Crocodile will
   manage to catch a juicy child for lunch?
   What might happen?

B. Talking around the story

1. The Enormous Crocodile's favourite food is juicy
   child. What is yours?
   What is your least favourite food? Why?

2. "It's something that walks on two legs."
   This is a sort of riddle. The answer is – "a child".
   Here is another riddle. "What is large and red
   and lies on its side in the gutter?" The answer
   is – "a dead bus".
   What other riddles do you know?

C. Activity: making a play

This story can be read like a play.
It needs four readers to take the parts –

> The Enormous Crocodile
> The Notsobig Crocodile
> Humpy-Rumpy
> The Narrator.

The Narrator's job is to read all the bits of the story
when nobody is actually speaking. This is the most

difficult part. To show where the Narrator has to speak we have printed his words in **darker type**.

First you should have a practice reading, with your teacher taking the Narrator's part. Three people from the class can take the other parts. Listen to how they read the story like a play.

Then work in groups of four. Decide in your group who is to play each part.
Decide on a good voice to use for your character.

With your group, read the story as a play.

When you have practised, perhaps you will be able to make a tape of your play on a tape-recorder. You could add sound effects, like jungle noises and the splashing of the water in the river.

2 Saturday by Seven

by Penelope Farmer

Penelope Farmer was the younger of twin sisters, so she grew up squabbling! By now, though, she and her sister are good friends. When Penelope was eight, she had to spend six months ill in bed. She passed the time reading and dreaming. She cannot remember a time when she did not write stories.

Now Penelope Farmer lives in a Victorian house with her husband, two children and a black pug dog called Alfred.

* * * * * * * * * * * *

It was Saturday morning and the sun was back at last after a week of rain. When Peter began his breakfast the sun just splashed the edge of the sink. By the time he was finished, it had crept across the kitchen to the table and a tongue of it lay warm on his plate. It made him feel happier. To please his mother he drank back a whole mug of milk. He waited till, sighing, she had folded her large newspaper. Only then did he ask, carefully and anxiously:

"Have you any jobs for me today, Mummy?" She paid him five pence for each job he did properly. Not for jobs like washing-up and making his bed, which he had to do anyway, but for extra jobs like weeding the garden.

"I should think so, love," she said. "There's always something needs doing."

"*Lots* of jobs?" asked Peter hopefully. But he felt his face turning warm and red.

"Peter's gone all red," his younger sister Lucy said. "Mummy, just look." She had tight fat plaits with sticking-out ends like toothbrushes, and Peter longed to tug at one. But that would only make his mother cross.

"Lucy, you just shut *up*," he said.

"*Lots* of jobs, Peter?" his mother asked. "How many do you mean?"

Peter dared not look at her but he could feel her eyes on him. He pushed his knife round and round his plate for something to do.

"Well – f-fifteen jobs, p'raps, or – or – nineteen – or twenty. *Lots* of jobs. You know, Mum."

"*Twenty* jobs?" asked Lucy, making her eyes round as peppermints.

"*Twenty* jobs?" asked his mother. "Why Peter – haven't you tried to earn any of that pound yet at *all?*"

Peter tapped on his plate with the knife. Without thinking he tapped a tune.

"N-no," he said miserably.

"And it has to be in by tonight?"

"Yes," he said.

"How long ago were you told about this camp, Peter?" his mother asked.

"Three – no four weeks," he mumbled.

"And what did I say when you asked to go?"

Peter grew cross. She knew the answers to her questions as well as he did. His tapping changed to a hard drum tapping, no tune at all, tap! tap! *tap!*

He said, "You told me I'd have to earn my own fare this time."

"Yes. And why?"

"Because it'd be the third camp I'd been on this summer and I couldn't always expect to be given everything."

"And isn't that fair?" she asked.

"Yes," muttered Peter, but he did not think so. He drove his knife so hard against his plate that Lucy squealed, "You'll *break* it, Peter." But his mother just went on looking at him.

"You *silly* old Peter. I'd have given you a job whenever you asked, only you never did. What about your pocket-money? Haven't you saved any of that?"

"No." For he had spent it all on sweets and pistol caps with his friend Thomas and the other boys. Four weeks before it had not seemed so difficult to earn a pound. He was always sure he could earn it by doing jobs for his mother. And he had thought that perhaps if he was lucky he might even earn it all at once with a reward for finding a dog or a diamond brooch. Or by winning a competition in a comic or on the back of a cornflakes packet.

Some people did. But he had not found any dogs or brooches and he had forgotten to keep the comics and the cornflake packets. And each day he had said to himself, "I'll start earning it tomorrow." Only he never had started.

That morning all he had in the world was three pence. But if he did not hand in a whole pound to the headmaster by seven o'clock that evening the camp bus would be off next weekend without him.

"Please, Mummy," he said miserably, "please, Mummy, I'd do all jobs specially well, honest I would . . . honest, *honest* I would."

His mother looked away out of the window, thinking. Peter had stopped even tapping with his knife. His hands waited, still and anxious as the rest of him.

But when she turned back to him at last she said, quite gently, "No, Peter, *no* I'm sorry. I can't give you twenty jobs today. I'll give you two, but you'll just have to find the rest for yourself if you can. It's your own fault for being such a silly and leaving it so late."

"Oh, Mummy!" Peter was horrified. He had been so certain that through her it would all come right.

* * * * * * * * * * * *

A. Talking about the story

1. When Peter first asks his mother for jobs to do, he is feeling very worried. The way he looks and acts shows this. Find the clues in the story which show that he is feeling worried.

2. Peter has only saved three pence since he heard about the camp.
   Why is this?

B. Talking around the story

1. Do you think Peter's mother is kind to him or not? Why do you give this answer?
   Is she being fair? Why, or why not?

2. Have you ever saved up for anything you really wanted?
   If so, what was it?
   How much did you save?
   How easy is it to save money?
   What are the best ways to save money?

3. Do you get pocket money?
   If you do, what do you spend it on?
   How much do you think someone of your age should get? Why?

C. Activity: rôle playing

Rôle-playing is acting. Soon you will go into pairs to act out a story. One person will be a child who wants money from one of his parents. The other will be the parent, who does not want to give the money. The child must give reasons why he wants the money. The parent must explain why he cannot have it.

Discuss with your teacher what these reasons might be.

Now act out this scene in pairs. Don't get angry with each other!

Perhaps when you have practised, some pairs can act out their scenes for the class.

3 Dinner Ladies Don't Count

by Bernard Ashley

Bernard Ashley is a teacher who works in London. He is headmaster of a junior school there. Sometimes children come up to him and ask shyly, "Mr Ashley, is your first name Bernard?" Then he knows that they have spotted one of his books in the library. He gives the school a copy of every one that is published.

"I don't make any fuss about my books with the children," he says. "But it is good for them to know that real books are written by ordinary people like me."

His wife, Iris, helps him a lot by reading what he has written. "Sometimes she advises me to write a bit again if she thinks I've hurried it. She's usually right," he says.

Bernard Ashley has three sons, who all enjoy writing too.

* * * * * * * * * * * *

Jason Paris stormed along Sutton Street. He pulled a fierce face at three girls strung across the pavement and turned left into the school playground. Inside, he kicked every plank in the fence and threw a stone at the huge rubbish bin. It clanged a warning to everyone. Jason had come to school with a smack instead of breakfast and they were all likely to feel the sting.

He barged backwards into the classroom. Miss Smith stopped smiling at Donna Paget's birthday cards. There they were, all love and kisses in her hands – but there was Jason knocking into chairs. There was a time and a place for everything, and she had to stop someone getting hurt.

"Hello, Jason. Do you want to use the Plasticine this morning?" she asked. Miss Smith knew the look, knew the sound of trouble.

"No!" Jason dug his hands into his pockets and glared at anyone foolish enough to look at him.

Donna Paget scooped up her birthday cards and pushed them hurriedly into her tray. "He spoils everything," she said.

"Would you like to read a book?" Miss Smith was asking.

Growling something in his throat, Jason cut a path through chairs and children to the book corner. He kicked a cushion and threw himself to the floor with a book. He could smell the dust in the hard, thin carpet. He felt the rough ridges beneath his elbows. It was a cheat, the book corner, he thought. It looked nice, but the floor and the books were too hard. He'd like to throw the books all round the room.

The book he had was big and flat and had sharp corners. It would be a good weapon. He stared at the shiny cover. All about dogs. Dogs! It would be about dogs! He twisted it in his hands like a bar bender in a circus, hoping it would bend and crack. But it was tougher than he was. Red in the face, he had to give up.

He stared at the poodle on the cover and he thought about his dog, Digger. Digger, small and tough, that got through little cracks and came back with bones. Digger, that let only him put his lead on, that trotted by his side and looked up when he talked to him.

Digger, that waited for him while he did things, that barked at people he wanted to frighten, and bit people he wanted bitten. That was his dog, Digger.

Poor Digger. Jason's stomach rolled with an empty feeling of loss. He felt sad – and to think that on top of that he'd had a hard smack, just for making a fuss about it!

Miss Smith didn't bother Jason with Maths but it was a lot of cutting out paper shapes: squares, triangles and circles. The gummed colours were stuck into Maths books, and the bits left over went into the bin. Everyone else was doing it.

With one half-closed eye Jason watched the activity, all the moving about for fresh colours, all the trips to the bin with the scraps. He watched and he waited until Donna Paget was up at the desk, part of a soft wall of good girls, hiding him from view.

* * * * * * * * * * * *

A. Talking about the story

1. Jason has been waiting till he is hidden from the teacher's view.
   What do you think he is going to do?
   Why do you think that?

2. Jason is in a very bad mood. Find two clues in the story that tell you *why* he is in a bad mood.

B. Talking around the story

1. From the story it sounds as if Digger is Jason's pet dog.
   Do you have a pet? If you do, what is it?
   What do you have to do to help look after it?
   Why do you think people like to have pets?

2. Jason is in a bad mood. Everybody has bad moods sometimes.
   What puts you in a bad mood?
   What do you do when you are in a bad mood?
   What puts your parents in a bad mood?
   What puts your teacher in a bad mood?

C. Activity: the birthday present game

Everyone needs a small piece of paper and a pencil.
On your paper write

1. Your name
2. One thing you would like to get for your next birthday.

Do not tell anyone what you write.
Then hand your paper to the teacher.

Your teacher will choose someone to be IT. The rest of the class take turns to ask IT questions to find out what ITS birthday present is.

Every question must begin with one of these
question words:

What . . . ?
Where . . . ?
Why . . . ?
How . . . ?
When . . . ?

You cannot, of course, ask "What is it?"

Everyone should listen carefully to all the questions
and the answers. If you think you have guessed
what ITS present is, put your hand up to tell the
teacher. If you cannot guess in four minutes, IT has
beaten the class.

You might have time for quite a few people to have
a turn at being IT.

4 Tales of a Fourth Grade Nothing
by Judy Blume

Judy Blume is an American
writer. She got the idea
for *Tales of a Fourth Grade
Nothing* from a newspaper
article about a little boy who
swallowed a pet turtle!
The character of Fudge is
based on her own son, Larry,
when he was that age.
But a lot of her stories
come from her own memory.
Judy Blume can remember
just about everything that
has happened to her since
she was eight years old.
This makes her a very good
writer for children.

This story is told by a boy called Peter Hatcher, who is in the fourth grade of an American primary school. He tells about his life, his parents, his pet turtle (Dribble), and his little brother Fudge. Fudge is only two-and-a-half years old, and he can be very naughty. . . .

I learned to stand on my head in gym class. I'm pretty good at it too. I can stay up for as long as three minutes. I showed my mother, my father and Fudge how I can do it right in the living-room. They were all impressed. Especially Fudge. He wanted to do it too. So I turned him upside down and tried to teach him. But he always tumbled over backwards.

Right after I learned to stand on my head Fudge stopped eating. He did it suddenly. One day he ate fine and the next day nothing. "No eat!" he told my mother.

She didn't pay too much attention to him until the third day. When he still refused to eat she got upset. "You've got to eat, Fudgie," she said. "You want to grow up to be big and strong, don't you?"

"No grow!" Fudge said.

That night my mother told my father how worried she was about Fudge. So my father did tricks for him while my mother stood over his chair trying to get some food into his mouth. But nothing worked. Not even juggling oranges.

Finally my mother got the brilliant idea of me standing on my head while she fed Fudge. I wasn't very excited about standing on my head in the kitchen. The floor is awfully hard in there. But my mother begged me. She said, "It's very important for Fudge to eat. Please help us, Peter."

So I stood on my head. When Fudge saw me upside down he clapped his hands and laughed. When he laughs he opens his mouth. That's when my mother stuffed some baked potato into it.

But the next morning I put my foot down. "No! I don't want to stand on my head in the kitchen. Or anywhere else!" I added. "And if I don't hurry I'll be late for school."

"Don't you care if your brother starves?"

"No!" I told her.

"Peter! What an awful thing to say."

"Oh . . . he'll eat when he gets hungry. Why don't you just leave him alone!"

That afternoon when I came home from school I found my brother on the kitchen floor playing with boxes of cereals and raisins and dried apricots. My mother was begging him to eat.

"No, no, no!" Fudge shouted. He made a terrible mess, dumping everything on the floor.

"Please stand on your head, Peter," my mother said. "It's the only way he'll eat."

"No!" I told her. "I'm not going to stand on my head any more." I went into my room and slammed the door. I played with Dribble until supper-time. Nobody ever worries about me the way they worry about Fudge. If I decided not to eat they'd probably never even notice!

That night during dinner Fudge hid under the kitchen table. He said, "I'm a doggie. Woof . . . woof . . . woof!"

It was hard to eat with him under the table pulling on my legs. I waited for my father to say something. But he didn't.

Finally my mother jumped up. "I know," she said. "If Fudgie's a doggie he wants to eat on the floor! Right?"

If you ask me Fudge never even thought about that. But he liked the idea a lot. He barked and nodded his head. So my mother fixed his plate and put it under the table. Then she reached down and petted him, like he was a real dog.

My father said, "Aren't we carrying this a little too far?" My mother didn't answer.

Fudge ate two bites of his dinner.

My mother was satisfied. . . .

The next day my mother dragged Fudge to Dr Cone's office. He told her to leave him alone. That Fudge would eat when he got hungry.

I reminded my mother that I'd told her the same thing – and for free! But I guess my mother didn't believe either one of us because she took Fudge to see three more doctors. None of them could find a thing wrong with my brother. One doctor even suggested that my mother cook Fudge his favourite foods.

So that night my mother broiled lamb chops just for Fudge. The rest of us ate stew. She served him the two little lamb chops on his plate under the table. Just the smell of them was enough to make my stomach growl. I thought it was mean of my mother to make them for Fudge and not for me.

Fudge looked at his lamb chops for a few

minutes. Then he pushed his plate away. "No!" he said. "No chops!"

"Fudgie . . . you'll starve!" my mother cried. "You *must* eat!"

"No chops! Cornflakes," Fudge said. "Want cornflakes!"

My mother ran to get the cereal for Fudge. "You can eat the chops if you want them, Peter," she told me.

I reached down and helped myself to the lamb chops. My mother handed Fudge his bowl of cereal. But he didn't eat it. He sat at my feet and looked up at me. He watched me eat his chops.

"*Eat your cereal!*" my father said.

"NO! NO EAT CEREAL!" Fudge yelled.

My father was really mad. His face turned bright red. He said, "Fudge, you will eat that cereal or you will wear it!"

This was turning out to be fun after all, I thought. And the lamb chops were really tasty. I dipped the bone in some ketchup and chewed away.

Fudge messed around with his cereal for a minute. Then he looked at my father and said, "NO EAT ... NO EAT ... NO EAT!"

My father wiped his mouth with his napkin, pushed back his chair, and got up from the table. He picked up the bowl of cereal in one hand, and Fudge in the other. He carried them both into the bathroom. I went along, nibbling on a bone, to see what was going to happen.

My father stood Fudge in the bath and dumped the whole bowl of cereal right over his head. Fudge screamed. He sure can scream loud.

My father motioned for me to go back to the kitchen. He joined us in a minute. We sat down and finished our dinner. Fudge kept on screaming. My mother wanted to go to him but my father told her to stay where she was. He'd had enough of Fudge's monkey business at meal times.

I think my mother really was relieved that my father had taken over. For once my brother got what he deserved. And I was glad!

A. Talking about the story

1. Fudge's mother tries lots of ways of getting Fudge to eat. What are they?

2. Peter does not seem to like Fudge very much. Find the things he says that tell you how he feels about his little brother.

B. Talking around the story

1. "Nobody ever worries about me the way they worry about Fudge."
Do you ever feel this about your family?
Why do you think Peter's mother worries more about Fudge than Peter?
What is the best position to be in a family — eldest, youngest, middle or only child?

2. Fudge's mother and father deal with him in very different ways. Which do you think was most sensible? Why?

3. When Fudge's father punishes him, he "makes the punishment fit the crime". What does this mean?
Think of some other bad things that children might do, and work out punishments to fit the crimes.

C. Activity: the message game

This is a game for the whole class.
Choose four people to send outside the room. Call them *A, B, C* and *D.* Perhaps they should take books to read because they may have to wait for a while.

The rest of the class should make up a recipe for a new food for Fudge to eat. Choose nice things to put in it so that he will want to eat it. Make sure that you all know exactly what to put in the food and how to make it. Your teacher can help you.

Then call *A* back into the classroom.
Your teacher will choose someone to explain to *A* exactly how to make the food. *A* may want to ask questions to make sure that he understands the recipe. When *A* understands, call in *B.*

A now explains the recipe to *B* without help from anyone else. *B* can ask *A* questions. When *B* understands, call in *C.*

B explains the recipe to *C* in the same way.

Last of all, *C* explains the recipe to *D.*

How different is the message now?
Why has the message changed?
You could try this game more than once, with different people going out each time. Try to end up with the message changed as little as possible.

Other Good Reads

1. *Superfudge* *** by Judy Blume (Piccolo)
   You know now what terrific trouble Fudge can
   cause. Peter reckons he's got quite enough to
   cope with already. So when his parents say that
   a new baby is on the way, it is enough to drive
   him almost round the bend. As well as this, it is
   time for Fudge to start school, and you can
   imagine the problems he causes there!

2. *Father Christmas* * and *Father Christmas Goes on
   Holiday* * by Raymond Briggs (Puffin)
   These are comic strip books with very little
   reading needed. This Father Christmas is a rather
   grumpy old man who's never quite satisfied
   with anything he does or anyone he meets. The
   pictures and the words together make two very
   funny books.

3. *The Magic Finger* * by Roald Dahl (Puffin)
   This funny book is by the same author as *The
   Enormous Crocodile*. It is about a girl who can
   point her magic finger at anyone she is angry
   with. Her finger punishes the people by making
   them change into strange creatures. Wouldn't
   it be fun to have a magic finger!

4. *Top of the World* ** by John Rowe Townsend
   (Puffin)
   Kathy and Donald are left to look after themselves for the day in their flat at the bottom of a
   tall block. But Donald breaks all the rules
   and climbs out on to the roof of the building.
   It is up to Kathy to try to rescue him and prevent
   a terrible accident.

5. *The Rocking Horse Secret* ** by Rumer Godden
   (Puffin)
   Tibby loves the old rocking horse, Noble, in
   Miss Pomeroy's house. But Miss Pomeroy's two
   greedy nieces refuse to believe that the old lady
   has really given Noble to Jill. They think
   everything in the house belongs to them . . .
   unless Miss Pomeroy's will can be found.

6. *Lucy* ** by Catherine Storr (Lions)
   Lucy wishes she was a boy because she thinks
   that boys always have more fun than girls. She
   isn't allowed to join the boys' gang, so she
   plans to search for an adventure of her own
   to prove she is as good as they are. Her chance
   comes when she sees three thieves stealing
   furniture from an empty house and decides to
   hide in the back of their van.

5 Clever Polly and the Stupid Wolf

by Catherine Storr

Catherine Storr started to write books for her three daughters. When one of them, Polly, was six or seven, she was really frightened of a wolf that she thought lived under her bed. Catherine Storr wrote *Clever Polly and the Stupid Wolf* to help her get over her fears. Now that her daughters are grown up, she also writes for adults. But she still enjoys writing for children.

This story is about a clever little girl called
Polly and a not-so-clever wolf who wants
to catch her and eat her up. The wolf tries
all sorts of tricks to trap Polly, but he
somehow never manages to get things
quite right.

One day he tries planting a grape pip
under Polly's window. He waits for it to
grow into a vine. Then he can climb up
the vine, get through the window and
catch Polly. Polly has to explain to him
that a vine takes years and years to grow.
So the wolf gives up this plan and goes off
to think up another one. . . .

About a week later Polly was sitting at the
drawing-room window again. She was sewing
and did not notice the wolf come into the
garden until she heard a sort of scrambling
noise outside. Then she looked out of the
window and saw the wolf very busy planting
something in the earth again.

"Good morning, Wolf," said Polly. "What
are you planting this time?"

"This time," said the wolf, "I've had a really
good idea. I'm planting something which will

grow up to your window in a moment."

"Oh," said Polly, interested. "What is that?"

"I have planted the rung of a ladder," said the wolf. "By tomorrow morning there'll be a long ladder stretching right up to your bedroom window. I specially chose a rung from the longest ladder I could see. A steeplejack was on the other end of it climbing a church steeple. He will be surprised when he comes down and finds the bottom rung of his ladder has gone. But in a very short time I shall be climbing in at your bedroom window, little Polly, and that will be the end of *you*."

Polly laughed. "Oh, poor Wolf, didn't you know that ladders don't grow from rungs or from anything else? They have to be made by men, and however many rungs you plant in this garden, even of steeplejacks' ladders, they won't grow into anything you could climb up. Go away, Wolf, and have a better idea, if you can."

The wolf looked very sad. He tucked his tail between his legs and trotted off along the road.

A week later Polly, who now knew what to expect, was sitting at the drawing-room window looking up and down the road.

"What are you waiting for?" asked her mother.

"I'm waiting for that stupid wolf," said Polly. "He's sure to come today. I wonder what silly idea he'll have got into his black head now?"

Presently the gate squeaked and the wolf came in carrying something very carefully in his mouth. He put it down on the grass and started to dig a deep hole.

Polly watched him drop the thing he had been carrying into the hole, cover it over with earth again, and stand back with a pleased expression.

"Wolf," called Polly, "what have you planted this time?"

"This time," replied the wolf, "you aren't going to escape. Have you read 'Jack and the Beanstalk', Polly?"

"Well, I haven't exactly read it," said Polly,

"but I know the story very well indeed."

"This time," said the wolf, "I've planted a bean. Now we know from the story of Jack that beans grow up to the sky in no time at all, and perhaps I shall be in your bedroom before it's light tomorrow morning, crunching up the last of your little bones."

"A bean!" said Polly, very much interested. "Where did it come from?"

"I shelled it out of its pod," said the wolf proudly.

"And the pod?" Polly asked. "Where did that come from?"

"I bought it in the vegetable shop," said the wolf, "with my own money," he added. "I bought half a pound, and it cost me a whole sixpence, but I shan't have wasted it because it will bring me a nice, juicy little girl to eat."

"You bought it?" said Polly. "Yourself, with your own money?"

"All by myself," said the wolf grandly.

"No one gave it to you?" Polly insisted.

"No one," said the wolf. He looked very proud.

"You didn't exchange it for anything?"
Polly asked again.

"No," said the wolf. He was puzzled.

"Oh, poor Wolf," said Polly pityingly. "You
haven't read 'Jack and the Beanstalk' at all.
Don't you know that it's only a *magic* bean
that grows up to the sky in a night, and you
can't buy magic beans. You have to be given

them by an old man in exchange for a cow or something like that. It's no good *buying* beans, that won't get you anywhere."

Two large tears dropped from the wolf's eyes.

"But I haven't *got* a cow," he cried.

"If you had you wouldn't need to eat me," Polly pointed out. "You could eat the cow. It's no good, Wolf, you aren't going to get me this time. Come back in a month or two, and we'll have a bean-feast off the plant you've just planted."

"I hate beans," the wolf sighed, "and I've got nearly a whole half-pound of them at home." He turned to go. "But don't be too cock-a-hoop, Miss Polly, for I'll get you yet!"

* * * * * * * * * * * *

A. Talking about the story

1. The wolf shows that he is stupid in many ways. What are they?

2. Polly is not at all frightened of the wolf. Find clues in the story which show you this.

B. Talking around the story

1. What animals frighten you?
   Do any other things frighten you?
   Sometimes, things seem more frightening than
   they do at other times. When are things more
   frightening?
   What do you do when you are frightened?

2. Have you ever planted a seed or tried to grow
   something?
   If so, what was it?
   Did it grow?
   Why do seeds sometimes not grow?

3. Animals cannot really speak, but in this story,
   the wolf talks like a person. Do you know any
   other stories where wolves can speak?
   What other stories do you know where animals
   can speak? Think of as many as you can.
   Do you like this sort of story? Why or why not?

C. Activity: story-telling

Think of a fairy story you know well.
Tell it to yourself in your mind. Your teacher will
give you a little while to do this.
Now you are going to work in pairs. Call yourselves
A and *B*.

First of all, *A* will be the story-teller, and *B* will be the listener. *A* tells the story to *B*, making it as exciting and interesting as possible. *B* listens carefully, and asks questions when the story is not clear. If *B* knows the story, he must make sure that *A* does not miss out any important bits.

When *A* has finished, swap over.
Now *B* is the story-teller, and should tell a different story in the same way. *A* listens and questions where necessary.

6 Chocolate Fever
by Robert Kimmel Smith

Robert Kimmel Smith gave up his job in advertising
to write full time in 1969. Since then he has written
three Sadie Shapiro books about a grandmother
who is the fastest knitter and the slowest jogger in
America, a suspense novel, two children's books
(including *Chocolate Fever*) and lots of plays and
television scripts. In the same time, he says, he has
also produced several thousand highly edible meals.
He lives with his wife and two teenage children in
a Victorian house in New York.

* * * * * * * * * * * * *

Henry Green loves chocolate and is
allowed to eat it almost non-stop. One
morning at school he notices that he is
covered in brown spots, which get larger
all the time. He is taken to hospital, where
he is found to have Chocolate Fever, a new
disease. The doctors and nurses surround
him – they are very interested in his
illness. But Henry is frightened. He panics
and runs away. . . .

It was almost two hours later now, and the sun was somewhat lower in the sky. Henry looked cautiously out of the garage, saw no one, and started on his way.

He walked for a long time, trying to stay on side streets and being careful to avoid attention. It was not easy. People kept staring at him. Henry ignored them and kept on walking.

In the middle of the street down which he was walking stood a school. Henry could see lots of boys playing in the schoolyard. He decided to walk through the yard to get to the next street. As he started through, all the boys stopped playing basketball and roller-skate hockey to look at him. It was as if all the noise and action had become frozen, like a movie or a TV show that stops suddenly.

Henry kept going. As he was about halfway through, just about in the middle of the yard, the kids seemed to come to life again. In less time than it takes to tell about it, he was surrounded.

Henry looked around him. All the boys

stared back. They had formed a tight circle around him. Henry didn't like it.

One of the tallest boys, who looked a good deal older than Henry, spoke up. "Boy, are you ugly!" he said.

"Yeah," said another boy in the crowd, "really ugly."

"Ugg-*ly!*" echoed another boy.

I'd better be polite, Henry thought. "Excuse me," he said in a quiet voice, "could I get through, please?"

The boys didn't move.

The big boy, who seemed to be a leader, spoke again. "I've seen pimples before, but those are ridiculous."

"They're not pimples," another boy said, "they're warts."

"Yeah, warts," said another, "they gotta be warts."

Now all the boys were speaking up.

"Ugliest warts in the whole world."

"In the world? Man, they are the ugliest warts in the universe!"

"I thought I seen ugly kids before, but this one is out of sight!"

"Horrible!"

"Disgusting!"

"Revolting!"

"And he smells, too," a fat boy with glasses said. "Yuch! Like a stupid sweet factory."

"Nauseating!"

The more the boys called him names, the worse Henry felt. He opened his mouth to say something, but nothing came out.

The big boy in the crowd held up his hands
to silence the others. "Quiet down, you guys,"
he said. "I want to talk to Mr Ugly here."

In a few moments the crowd was silent.

"Now then," the big one said, "you – Mr
Ugly – what's your name, kid?"

Before Henry answered, he thought carefully. He was ashamed of himself and the way he looked. But he was even more ashamed of the gang around him. How dare they act so mean? He hadn't harmed them. And now, when he could certainly use a friend, they had clearly marked him as an enemy.

Henry got angry, but he kept his anger firmly under control.

"My name is my own business," he said. "It's no concern of yours."

The gang hooted and shouted at Henry's reply. A few even whistled.

"Don't be fresh, kid," the big boy said. "We don't like fresh kids here."

A few of the larger boys edged closer to Henry, closing the ring around him tighter.

"Let me hit him, Frankie," a voice said.

"Let me get him," another boy said.

Henry thought quickly. "Touch me and you die," he said. "I have a rare and mysterious disease. Whoever touches me will catch it and die a horrible death!"

A. Talking about the story

1. What does the leader of the gang look like?
   What is his name?

2. Look back at the story and pick out all the things
   he says.
   Do you like him? Why?

3. This story is set in America, and it was written
   by an American author. Americans speak
   English, but they often use special American
   words and expressions. Go through the passage
   and pick out as many "Americanisms" as you
   can.

B. Talking around the story

1. Why did the gang pick on Henry?
   How do you think Henry felt when they ganged
   up on him?
   What is it like to be bullied?
   Do you know of any people who have been
   bullied because of the way they look? What do
   you think about that?

2. Henry has got Chocolate Fever from eating too
   much chocolate. What other nice foods could

people eat too much of?
Think up some good names for illnesses they
could get from eating too much of these foods.

C. Activity: introducing yourself

When Henry meets the gang, they ask him, "What's
your name, kid?"
They want to know who he is and what he is like.
Often when you meet new people, they want to
know about you. You have to introduce yourself.

Work in pairs. Call yourselves *A* and *B*. Pretend that
you do not know each other.
A must introduce himself to *B*. He should give
name, age, address, and some information about
himself and his family. *A* could also mention
hobbies and interests, favourite games and foods,
and favourite subjects at school.

Then swap over. In the same way, *B* should
introduce himself to *A*.

When you have finished, your teacher will call the
class together. She will ask a few people to
introduce themselves to the whole class.

Talk about how your introductions could be made
more interesting.

7 Lion at Large
by Richard Parker

Richard Parker has a wife, five children and a 1933
Rolls Royce. He likes to grow a beard every winter,
but he shaves it off in the spring. He has been a
reporter, a librarian, a postman, a pig-farmer, a
factory hand and a secretary to a well-known
author. He has also been a teacher.

Richard Parker has travelled a lot, first in the
Services during the Second World War, and later
for his work and because he likes it. He has lived in
Tasmania, which is an island off the south coast of
Australia.

* * * * * * * * * * * *

Barry wakes up in the middle of the night
and looks out of his bedroom window.
And there, standing by the gate, is a lion!
Barry watches it in horror for a while,
until it moves off into the darkness. Then
he wonders what to do. Should he wake
his father and tell him? Barry decides not
to wake him. Instead, he will get up early
the next morning and tell his father before
he goes to work. . . .

Unfortunately when Barry did wake up the following morning his father had already left for work.

"Get up now and you won't have to rush your breakfast," his mother said.

Barry jumped straight out of bed. "Mum, is Dad up?"

"Of course he is. And gone to work."

"But I had something important to tell him."

"It'll have to wait till this evening, then," said his mother, already half-way out of the room.

"Wait a minute – "

"I've got the bacon on; I can't," she said. "Put clean socks on; I've left them on your chair."

Barry pursued her to the kitchen. "But, Mum, listen," he said. "I saw a lion out of the window last night. Just wandering about in the road it was. Then it went right down through the orchard."

"Oh really, Barry," said his mother. "Look at you, still in your pyjamas. Go and get dressed this very minute."

"But, Mum, didn't you hear what I said?"

"Get your clothes on first. Then I'll listen," said his mother.

Barry went back to his bedroom. He pulled off his pyjama jacket and threw it as hard as he could on the floor. Then he thumped the bed with his clenched fists eight or nine times. After that he felt better and got dressed. He made his bed and went through into the other room for breakfast. He did not say anything else to his mother until they were both sitting at the table.

"Mum," he said, "you didn't hear what I said about last night, did you?"

"No, what did you say?"

"Well, I woke up in the night, you see – "

"I knew you would," said his mother. "You had far too much supper."

"Oh, Mum. *Please!*"

"Well, go on, then."

Barry told his mother exactly what had happened and what he had seen out of the

bedroom window. His mother went on eating for a moment, and then she said, "Do you want another slice of bread?"

"Yes," said Barry. "I mean, no."

"Well, make up your mind."

"But what do you think about it, Mum?"

"About what?"

"About the lion," said Barry. "I've just been telling you!"

"I know, and you don't have to shout at me."

"But you haven't said what you think."

"What do you expect me to say? It must

have been very exciting for you. Was it a very big lion?"

"I thought so at first, but that was probably just the way the moon was shining. Afterwards it seemed about the usual size."

"I see," said Barry's mother. "Just an ordinary lion. With a mane?"

"Of course it had a mane," said Barry. "Otherwise it would have been a lioness."

"You're dropping marmalade on the cloth," she said. "Do try to be careful; it was clean on only yesterday."

Barry scraped up the marmalade with his knife.

"But don't you think it was exciting?" he cried.

"Well, I said so, didn't I?"

"Yes, but you don't look excited."

Barry's mother laughed. "You are a funny boy. What did you expect me to do? Scream? Faint? Throw a fit?"

"I thought you might want to phone the police or something," said Barry. "That's why

I wanted to tell Dad; he could have gone into the station on his way to work."

"Oh, Barry," his mother said, smiling. "Really!"

Barry knew what that meant. "But I did see a lion," he said. "Cross my heart. I really and truly did. I'm not making it up."

"Of course you saw one," she said soothingly. "But it couldn't have been a real one, could it? It must have been a dream. Now do be sensible. A big boy of almost ten – "

"I don't see what being almost ten has got to do with it," cried Barry angrily. "At least, I'm old enough to know when I've seen something and when I haven't. How do you know whether it was a dream or not? You weren't there. You were asleep."

"Now you're being rude," said his mother sharply.

"Well, it's enough to make anybody rude," said Barry.

"I think we'd better say no more about it," said his mother, getting up from the table and beginning to clear away.

"But that's jolly unfair," Barry cried. "Look, I'll prove I'm telling the truth. I think you're being absolutely beastly – "

"Barry!" said his mother sharply. "You're being very childish. I think the best thing you can do is to go into your bedroom for ten minutes and calm down. When you feel like coming out and apologising for being so rude to me – "

Barry did not wait to hear any more, but ran into his bedroom and slammed the door behind him.

* * * * * * * * * * * *

A. Talking about the story

1. Barry's mother does not believe he has really seen a lion. What does she say and do that shows you this?

2. When she does not believe him, Barry is angry. What clues in the way he acts and speaks show that he is angry?

B. Talking around the story

1. Barry really *has* seen a lion. What do you think he should do now?
   How can he make people believe him?

2. Adults quite often do not believe children.
   Why is this?
   Have you ever told a true story and someone has not believed you?
   If you have, what was it? How did you feel?
   Have you ever told a lie and someone has believed you?
   If you have, what was it? How did you feel?

3. So far in this book there have been three stories with mothers in them. They are *Saturday by Seven, Tales of a Fourth Grade Nothing*, and *Lion at Large*.
   Look back at the stories.
   Which mother do you like best? Why?
   Which do you like least? Why?
   What do you think makes "a good mum"?

C. Activity: description

Work in groups of about four.
Each person in the group should think of a wild animal. Don't tell anyone else what it is.

Think about:
    1. what it looks like;
    2. how it moves;
    3. what noise it makes;
    4. where it lives;
    5. what it eats.

Take it in turns to describe your animal to the rest
of the group. Do not mention what the animal is.
No one must try to guess while you are speaking —
they must keep quiet till you are finished. When
each person has finished describing an animal,
the others in the group should guess what the
animal is.

Other Good Reads

1. *Jim and the Beanstalk* * by Raymond Briggs (Puffin)
   The wolf in *Clever Polly* is quite different from the wolf in *Little Red Riding Hood* — so is the giant in *Jim and the Beanstalk* quite different from the giant in *Jack and the Beanstalk*. Jim finds that an enormous plant has sprouted up overnight outside his window. He climbs up and finds, not a fearsome ogre, but a toothless, almost hairless, short-sighted (but rich) giant who needs his help.

2. *The Village Dinosaur* ** by Phyllis Arkle (Puffin)
   When a live dinosaur (Dino) is hauled out of the chalk pit, he is bound to cause some changes in a peaceful village. His enormous size and small brain create a lot of trouble and fun.

3. *Littlenose* * by John Grant (BBC Publications)
   Littlenose is a boy from the Ice Age, which was a very long time ago. He often gets into trouble and danger because he does silly things like letting the fire go out, or being trapped by the tide. Fortunately, his pet mammoth, Two-Eyes, usually manages to rescue him in time.

The boys in the next two books look somewhat "unusual", like Henry Green in *Chocolate Fever*.

4. *The Boy Who Sprouted Antlers*** by John Yeoman (Lions)
   Billy's teacher claims that he can do anything if he puts his mind to it. Billy rather likes the idea of being able to do anything, and when Melanie and Paul challenge him to grow horns, he decides to try. The results amaze everyone.

5. *Flat Stanley** by Jeff Brown (Methuen Magnet)
   Stanley Lambchop is a perfectly normal small boy except that he is only half an inch thick. This is because once, when he was asleep, a giant notice board fell on him. Stanley has enormous fun squeezing into places other boys can't get to, but he does come across some problems. . . .

6. *The Worried Ghost**** by Seymour Reit (Scholastic Book Services)
   You don't expect to meet a ghost on a school outing, but that is exactly what happens to Andy. What is more, he makes friends with the ghost and tries to help him find the missing letter. Only the letter will allow the poor ghost to rest in peace.

8 Hide Till Daytime
by Joan Phipson

Joan Phipson is from Australia. The story of *Hide Till Daytime* is set in Sydney, which is a big city in Australia. Joan lives 288 kilometres from Sydney, on a farm where she keeps sheep and cattle. When she was younger she used to travel the world.

* * * * * * * * * * * *

Agatha Pepper and her little brother George are out shopping with their mum and dad in a big department store. It is very crowded and the two children get lost among the shoppers. Mr Pepper thinks his wife is looking after the children, so he goes back to the office. Mrs Pepper thinks her husband is looking after them, so she goes back home. So when darkness falls and the store closes for the night, Agatha and George are left there alone.

In the quiet, empty store, Agatha manages to find the way back to the chicken counter, where she last saw her parents . . . .

It took her a long time to realise that the floor
was empty of all but the cleaners. It was night
time. The chickens had been put away, the spit
turned off and everyone gone home. Mr and
Mrs Pepper had gone home too.

George had been smelling the remains of the
cooking smells and now he said loudly, "I'm
hungry."

At first Agatha could think of nothing but
that her mother and father had gone home,
leaving them behind. She could not believe it
and began hunting round the other counters in
case they should be there still. But they weren't,
and at last she had to realise that they had,
indeed, left without their children. She would
not have believed it possible. A terribly lost,
hollow feeling started to creep up from the
middle of her stomach. It made her cold all
over, and shivery. It was George saying again
that he was hungry that made her remember
that she was nine. She must still look after
George – more than ever, now he had no one
but her. And it was still her fault that they

were here. She began to wonder if her mother
and father had been so angry that they could
no longer bear the sight of her. Perhaps this
was why they had left. A tear trickled down
her cheek and bounced on to the chicken
counter.

George had been looking round at all the
food that still lay piled up on the counters. But
now he pulled at her hand and turned to look
at her. She took a great breath, swallowed, and
quickly wiped her wet cheek on her sleeve.

"Well, if you're hungry we must find you
something lovely to eat, mustn't we? There's
plenty here."

George's face had been an alarming mixture
of anger, greed and fear. But now it was
suddenly transformed by a wide and sunny
smile.

"Goody," he said. "There's cakes."

"Come on then," said Agatha. "We'll see
what we can find and you shall eat as much as
you want." Now that George had no one but
her, she had to take the risk that it might be

stealing. It was her fault he was hungry and without parents, and she would give him as much to eat as she was able.

In the end it was George's stomach that was not able. They had found their way in among the cakes. All the glass cases were open at the back and there were plenty for them to choose

from. There were all kinds – sponge, cinnamon, chocolate, caramel, strawberry, nut. Most of them were filled with a kind of cream that both of them thought the loveliest thing they had

ever tasted until about the third cake. When
they had finished that they decided they would
never eat that sort of cream again.

There was plenty more to eat on other
counters – cheese, fruit, biscuits and endless
boxes of chocolates. But none of it looked as
delicious as it had before. George, his mouth
wreathed with chocolate, was quiet and dreamy.
Agatha knew that they must now leave the
shop and try to find Wynyard Station. Someone would tell them which train to catch.
Someone would have to tell them the way to
Wynyard Station, too. After that she knew the
way home. And, more important, she knew
the way out from the Food Hall.

"Come on, Georgie," she said. "We'll go
home now."

They walked hand in hand up the wide stairs
to the doorway where they had come in. She
pushed first one door and then another. She
pushed all the doors in turn, but none would
open. She was just trying to remember how to
find her way to the side door, which she knew

was somewhere there, when George said,
"I feel sick."

"Don't be silly, George. It's just because
you're tired." It was what her mother had
sometimes said. But she looked at George's
face and saw that all the red had gone from
his cheeks. They were now a yellowy-green
colour. "Come on then. Quick," she said. "And
don't be sick until I get you to the bathroom."

She knew where it was – up the stairs for
several flights and into the door on the landing.

They got there just in time. George was sick
in a very lavish way while Agatha held him.
When she had finally got him mopped up he
yawned, shivered and started to cry with a
high, mewing sound like a kitten. He seemed
to have crumpled and gone strangely bendy. It
was no use trying to get him to Wynyard
Station in the state he was in now. He yawned
again, between sobs. It was his bedtime. It was
at this moment that Agatha had her brainwave.

* * * * * * * * * * * *

A. Talking about the story

1. What do you think Agatha's brainwave might be?

2. Agatha has been left in charge of George. She does not want him to be frightened. What things does she do to stop him from getting too frightened?

B. Talking around the story

1. Which big department stores have you been to? What did you go to buy?

   If *you* were locked in a big department store all night, what would you do?

   How could you try to escape? If you could not escape, where would you sleep?

   How would you amuse yourself?

2. Do you think Agatha and George were right to eat the cakes? Give your reasons for your answer. If you could have your pick of all the things displayed in a department store, what would you choose?

3. Agatha is very upset when she finds her parents have gone.

   Have you ever been lost?

   If you have, where was it? What happened?

C. Activity: giving directions

When someone is lost, they have to ask for directions to find their way home. Someone has to give them directions. It is important to be able to give directions clearly.

Work with a partner. One of you is *A* and one of you is *B*.

A should ask for directions from the place you are now to somewhere else in the school (for example, "How do I get to the headteacher's room?" or "How do I get from here to the main gate?").

B must give clear directions to the places *A* has asked about. If you are *A*, you should pretend that you really do not know the way. You should listen carefully and ask questions when *B* is not clear.

A should ask for directions to about three or four different places.

Then swap over. This time *B* should ask for directions to places a bit further away (for example, "How do I get from here to the nearest bus stop?" or "How do I get to the nearest sweet shop?").

A must give clear directions, while *B* listens and asks questions when *A* is not clear.

9 The Worst Witch
by Jill Murphy

Jill Murphy went to a girls' convent school. Perhaps she has used some of the things that happened to her there in her book about a school for witches.

She lives in London with her grey furry dog Lottie, whom she rescued from a barn in Scotland. Lottie has become famous since she appeared in a television series called "The Bagthorpe Saga".

Jill likes to go cycling on Hampstead Heath with Lottie, who runs along beside her. But she has a new hobby too — rollerskating. So if you see someone on bright yellow and blue rollerskates, speeding along with a big furry dog, it's probably her.

* * * * * * * * * * * *

Miss Cackle's Academy for Witches stood at the top of a high mountain surrounded by a pine forest. It looked more like a prison than a school, with its gloomy grey walls and turrets. Sometimes you could see the pupils on their broomsticks flitting like bats above the playground wall, but usually the place was half

hidden in mist, so that if you glanced up at the
mountain you would probably not notice the
building was there at all.

Everything about the school was dark and
shadowy: long, narrow corridors and winding
staircases – and of course the girls themselves,
dressed in black gymslips, black stockings,
black hob-nailed boots, grey shirts and black-
and-grey ties. Even their summer dresses were
black-and-grey checked. The only touches of
colour were the sashes round their gymslips –
a different colour for each house – and the
school badge, which was a black cat sitting on
a yellow moon. For special occasions, such as

prize-giving or Hallowe'en, there was another
uniform consisting of a long robe worn with a
tall, pointed hat, but as these were black too,
it didn't really make much of a change.

There were so many rules that you couldn't
do *any*thing without being told off, and there
seemed to be tests and exams every week.

Mildred Hubble was in her first year at the
school. She was one of those people who
always seem to be in trouble. She didn't
exactly mean to break rules and annoy the
teachers, but things just seemed to *happen*
whenever she was around. You could rely on
Mildred to have her hat on back-to-front or
her bootlaces trailing along the floor. She
couldn't walk from one end of a corridor to
the other without someone yelling at her, and
nearly every night she was writing lines or
being kept in (not that there was anywhere to
go if you were allowed out). Anyway, she had
lots of friends, even if they did keep their
distance in the potion laboratory, and her best
friend Maud stayed loyally by her through

everything, however hair-raising. They made
a funny pair, for Mildred was tall and thin
with long plaits which she often chewed
absent-mindedly (another thing she was told
off about), while Maud was short and tubby,
had round glasses and wore her hair in bunches.

On her first day at the academy each pupil
was given a broomstick and taught to ride it,
which takes quite a long time and isn't nearly
as easy as it looks. Half-way through the first
term they were each presented with a black
kitten which they trained to ride the
broomsticks.

Poor Mildred Hubble is very worried about the presentation of the kittens. She is sure something will go wrong for her. And, sure enough, when it is her turn to get a kitten, she finds that there are no black ones left. All Mildred gets is a rather dim-looking tabby kitten with white paws. She doesn't think it will, be easy to train it to ride on her broomstick . . .

It had taken Mildred several weeks of falling off and crashing before she could ride the broomstick reasonably well, and it looked as though her kitten was going to have the same trouble. When she put it on the end of the stick, it just fell off without even trying to hold on. After many attempts, Mildred picked up her kitten and gave it a shake.

"Listen!" she said severely. "I think I shall have to call you Stupid. You don't even *try* to hold on. Everyone else is all right – look at all your friends."

The kitten gazed at her sadly and licked her nose with its rough tongue.

"Oh, come on," said Mildred, softening her voice. "I'm not really angry with you. Let's try again."

And she put the kitten back on the broomstick, from which it fell with a thud.

Maud was having better luck. Her kitten was hanging on grimly upside down.

"Oh, well," laughed Maud. "It's a start."

"Mine's useless," said Mildred, sitting on the broomstick for a rest.

"Never mind," Maud said. "Think how hard it must be for them to hang on by their claws."

An idea flashed into Mildred's head, and she dived into the school, leaving her kitten chasing a leaf along the ground and the broomstick still patiently hovering. She came out carrying her satchel which she hooked over the end of the broom and then bundled the kitten into it. The kitten's astounded face peeped out of the bag as Mildred flew delightedly round the yard.

A. Talking about the story

1. Miss Cackle's Academy for Witches "looked more like a prison than a school." In what ways does it look like a prison? What other places does the description of the school remind you of?

2. Describe what the uniform at Miss Cackle's Academy looked like.

3. How did Mildred manage to make her kitten stay on her broomstick?

B. Talking around the story

1. Do you think Mildred's idea for making the kitten stay on the broomstick is cheating? What does cheating mean? Is it possible to cheat in any game you play in the playground? Which games? How do people cheat? What happens to them when they do?

2. Do you have a uniform at your school? If you do, do you like it? Why, or why not? If you don't, would you like one? Why? Why do many schools want children to wear uniforms? Do you agree with their reasons?

C. Activity: group discussion

You have already done a lot of discussion work with your teacher. Now you are going to have discussions in small groups on your own. Everyone should have a chance to speak. There must be some rule which will give everyone their turn. With your teacher, decide on some good rules for your discussion groups. Perhaps you will need to put one person in the group in charge of the discussion.

When you are ready, divide into groups of about four. You will need a piece of paper and a pencil for making notes. You are going to discuss "School Rules".
First, think of the rules that you have at your school. Think of as many as you can. One of the group should make a list.
Go through your list, and work out the reasons for each rule. Talk about whether you agree with the reasons.
Then think of any other rules that might make life better at your school. Talk about these with your group. Does everyone agree?

When you have finished, your teacher can call the class together. Perhaps you will have time for each group to tell the class what you think of the rules you have, and any new rules you have thought up.

10 A Pony in the Luggage

by Gunnel Linde

Gunnel Linde comes from
Sweden. Her father died
when she was only six
months old, and from then
on, she and her mother
lived in a little flat. She was
very fond of her many dolls
and teddy bears, which used
to get stuck in between the
blankets of her bed. She
wrote her first story for her
teddy bears. When she grew
up and had children,
Gunnel Linde started to
write children's books.
Now she is also a television
producer, making children's
programmes.

> Nicholas and Anna are on holiday with
> their aunt in Denmark. They have won a
> small pony (Danny) in a lottery at the zoo,
> but they are afraid that they won't be
> allowed to keep him. However, they are
> sure that once their parents see the pony
> they'll love him – so they decide to try to
> smuggle him home. But first they'll have
> to hide him in their hotel room till the
> holiday is over. Anna keeps their aunt
> talking on the balcony while Nicholas
> tries to get Danny up to the hotel bedroom
> without being spotted. . . .

Nicholas turned round on the red carpet and
saw himself in all the mirrors. Whatever had
Anna done with the pony? Just then there was
a sort of snuffling noise from the other side of
the reception desk. Nicholas stretched across
the desk and looked down. There he was, the
world's sweetest pony, and his tail was so long
that it touched the floor. Nicholas climbed over
the desk and gave Danny a welcoming pat.
And Danny nudged his hand and nodded. He
was really no bigger than a St Bernard dog.
Now, the question was how to get him upstairs.

Nicholas took him by the mane and made encouraging noises. Danny allowed himself to be led as far as the stairs, but there he stopped and looked doubtful. "Come on, surely you can walk up ordinary stairs," said Nicholas.

Danny hesitated and looked as though he wondered if he really could. But then he sighed and started plodding up the stairs. When they reached the top, they came to a corridor with rows of doors on either side. How could they get past without meeting anybody? Nicholas clenched his fist. "Typical," he muttered.

"They tell you all about horses as vertebrate animals and what kind of teeth they have and so on and so forth. Biology books are just full of the stuff. But not a word about useful things like how to get a pony upstairs into a hotel bedroom."

One of the doors in the corridor was open and Nicholas could hear a chambermaid humming to herself as she worked. He crept towards the door, hoping that he would be able to close it. And then he caught sight of a pile of blankets. He cautiously stretched out his hand and pulled a blanket towards him. It might come in handy. Suddenly he heard footsteps as the other end of the corridor. There was only one thing he could do. He unfolded the blanket and draped it over Danny so that not even his head was showing.

It was the porter. He stopped in front of Nicholas with a stern expression on his face.

"Where are you off to?" he said. Nicholas tried to sound nonchalant.

"I'm going to Room 119. We live there."

"And what's this then?" The porter pointed at the bundle of blanket that was Danny.

Nicholas swallowed. "This? Oh, this – well you see, it's Danny, my brother," he said. "We're playing horses. Gee up, Dan. Come along."

The porter looked at the disobedient bundle of blanket. "He doesn't seem to be very well trained yet. He won't do what you tell him," he said, laughing. "Off you go, up to your room; you mustn't carry on like this in the corridors. The hotel blankets aren't here for you to play with, you know."

Nicholas wanted to go at once, but Danny wouldn't budge. He just stood there under the blanket. "Come on, Danny, off we go." Nicholas felt desperate. All would be well if Danny kept quiet, but of course he didn't. He let out a funny neighing sound.

"Would you believe it," said the porter. "Quite a good imitation. Not bad at all. He ought to go on the stage, your brother." The porter was just about to pat Danny through the blanket, but fortunately at that moment Danny decided to move off, followed anxiously by Nicholas.

"Well I'm blessed, the things children get up to. You might almost think it was a real horse."

Nicholas led Danny past Auntie's door and into his own room. He turned the key twice in the lock.

"Quiet now, Danny, while I make you a stable in the cupboard," he said.

A. Talking about the story

1. Nicholas tries to make Danny move in several ways.
   Look through the story and say what they are.

2. Look again at the part of the story where the
   porter arrives and speaks to Nicholas. What kind
   of person do you think he is? Do you like him?
   Why?

B. Talking around the story

1. Anna and Nicholas have won the pony in a lottery.
   What animal would you like to win? Why?
   Do you think your parents would be pleased if
   you had won this animal? Explain why or why not.

2. When the porter asks Nicholas who Danny is,
   he tells him that Danny is his brother.
   Do you think Nicholas is right to tell that lie?
   Give reasons for your answer.
   Could he have said anything else that would not
   make the porter suspicious?
   What would you have done if you had been
   Nicholas?

3. What problems do you think Nicholas and Anna
   will have when they try to keep the pony in a
   cupboard in their hotel room?

C. Activity: group discussion

You are going to have another discussion in small
groups. First of all, talk over with your teacher how
the group discussion went last time. What
problems did you have? With your teacher, work
out ways to solve these problems. If you need to,
work out new rules to help your group discussion
go well.

Then split into groups of about five.
You will need a paper and pencil.
You are going to discuss "What is the best kind of
holiday?"
First of all, think of all the different types of holiday
people can go on (for example, a seaside hotel, a
holiday on a farm, a camping holiday in a tent, and
so on). One of the group should note these down
as you think of them.

Then talk in your group about the good and bad
points about each sort of holiday.

After your discussion, have a vote to find out which
kind of holiday your group thinks is best.

Your teacher will call the class together and ask one
person from each group to tell the rest of the class
what you have decided.

Other Good Reads

1. *Burglar Bill* * by Janet and Allan Ahlberg
   (Picture Lions)
   Burglar Bill spends a most successful night
   stealing. Part of his booty is a large cardboard
   box with holes in it. Later he discovers that it
   contains a real live baby. Whose baby is it? Can
   he look after it? And what happens when a
   burglar gets burgled?

2. *The Worst Witch Strikes Again**** by Jill Murphy
   (Puffin)
   If you've enjoyed reading about Mildred's
   problems in *The Worst Witch*, you will certainly
   get a lot of fun out of this sequel. Mildred is to
   look after the new girl, Enid Nightshade. The
   idea is that it will turn her into a responsible
   member of the school, but somehow Enid's
   naughtiness and Mildred's bad luck lead them
   into endless trouble.

3. *Gobbolino, the Witch's Cat* ** by Ursula Moray
   Williams (Puffin)
   Gobbolino was born a witch's cat, but does not
   want to do wicked things all the time. He just
   wants to belong to an ordinary family and be
   loved by them. But he soon finds that life is not
   as simple as that for a witch's cat.

4. *The Penny Pony* ** by Barbara Willard (Puffin)
Cathy and Roger have always wanted a pony.
This adventure begins when they find a model
pony in a junk shop and buy him for a penny.
But will a penny pony be as good as a real one?

5. *A Dog and a Half* *** by Barbara Willard (Knight)
Jill's tortoise dies. She and her friend, Limpet,
want another pet, preferably a huge dog. But
Jill's father laughingly says she can only have a
dog if she can find one for the price of a tortoise.
It seems impossible, but then they are given
Brandy, an enormous St Bernard, who turns out
to be "a dog and a half" in more ways than one!

6. *It's Too Frightening For Me* * by Shirley Hughes
(Puffin)
We hope this book isn't too frightening for you!
It's about Jim and Arthur, two boys who like to
hang about a big gloomy house wondering what
is inside. Then one day a white face appears at
the window. It is a young girl. She beckons to
them silently to come in, and then disappears . . .